The only Budget Book

you will ever need and thank
goodness for that!

Lauren A. Welch, AFC

Thrive Financial Counseling, LLC

The Only Budget Book

*you will ever need and
thank goodness for that!*

By

Lauren A. Welch, AFC
Thrive Financial Counseling, LLC.

The Only Budget Book

Copyright 2015 Lauren A. Welch
Published by Lauren A. Welch
Cover Art by Chris & Design, Inc.
Formatting Services by Wizards in Publishing

I understand the dreaded B (b...b...b...) B word. I get it. It is a nasty word in most houses. I hope to turn it into something trusted, loved, and respected in your house, like the family dog. There will be information as well as reflection and work. Just like anything else, information is no good unless it is understood and used. Game plan? **Let's get to it.**

So, what is a budget?

First, a direct, straight from a dictionary definition: Budget as a noun: an estimate of income and expenses for a set period of time, *keep within the household budget*. Budget as an adjective: inexpensive, "a budget trip".

What do I think a budget is? *A document that is forever, living, breathing and changing.* It is not constricting but freeing. This document outlines what your money does throughout the month, based on what you tell it to do. We will come back and talk about both of these ideas again (as they are both powerful and very important!)

Okay, but why do we need a budget?

I have worked with hundreds and hundreds of people; families, singles, military, people filing bankruptcy, high school students, senior citizens, those below the poverty level, college students and everyone in between. I believe 1000% that every person, no matter their situation (and most of the time, their excuse!) has to start their financial success journey with a budget.

A high school student only makes $75 dollars a week. His parents help with his basic living expenses but he has to pay for gas, insurance and fun money. His gas is $100 a month and his portion of his parents' insurance is $50. That allows for an additional $150 a month in fun money. Does he really need a budget? Yes! He needs to start saving. Savings for college, savings for trips, savings for emergencies, savings for "fun" outside of his monthly *income*. What if he loses his job or decides to quit working? *How will he afford his bills?* I would suggest he set-aside an amount each month for fun and the rest for savings. Even with a few budget categories, **he still needs a written budget and a tracking system**. This prepares him for how he will need to budget when he has more money and more budget categories in the future.

A budget gives you and yours a control over the money you have earned. There is nothing worse than working hard, earning money and wondering where it went. A budget allows you to utilize your hard earned money for longer through the use of savings, investing and other goals that are not available without a hand in the process.

If budgets are so important, why don't some people have them?

Like I stated above, I have worked with people from all walks of life and I have received many answers for why people do not have budgets.

I present to you my budget myth roll call:

Myth: I just don't have the time.

Fact: **I won't sugarcoat it; you are reading a book about budgeting that includes homework and projects. Anything worth doing takes time, right?** Cliché, but true. Building the foundation for successful household finances and setting up a successful budget *will take time*. The first few months will be filled with tracking, getting used to having a budget, and making changes to not only your budget, but also the way you handle money. What is after that? You might spend an hour a month, a few minutes every few days, and five to ten minutes at the end of the month to review.

While at the doctor's office recently, there was a comic of a doctor telling his patient, *"you can either fit an hour into your busy schedule to exercise or you can be dead 24 hours a day."* Not completely relevant here but, *fitting in personal finance is as important as anything else.* **If you work, be responsible for the money you earn.** Just like we were given bodies to take care of, we should take care of our financial bodies, the money we have, today and in the future, so like our bodies, will last longer and feed us into retirement. Spend the time with good-for-you vegetables like budgets (stick with me here...) and time in cardio-like budget tracking to be successful.

Myth: They just don't work for me. (I cannot figure them out, they are too difficult, we don't work that way...)

Fact: Any way you slice it, the myth is a budget is for a certain type of person or a person with a certain kind of skills. Since a budget is living, moving and changing *(we have heard this already, haven't we?),* a budget is also flexible in how it is done (as long as it is!). We will talk about this in more detail later in the book but, **budgets need to be written and understandable, useful and realistic to you**. Outside of that, do what works for you.

Myth: Budgets are too constricting, I feel like I am being choked or drowning.

Fact: I feel this is true of budgets at first, especially if you have never done them before or never done them right. A budget is meant to categorize your spending and keep your spending to the amount you decided. $50 for eating out for the month, for example. For a first time budgeter that seems like, what my husband said *years* ago, "a straitjacket." **That amount is what you make it, BUT needs to be: realistic both for your income and your spending habits.** Once you get used to your budget and your new spending plan, you will see the fruits of your labors and see what beautiful things can come from spending wisely.A budget will feel like you can breathe again and move. You will feel like you have a new financial life. **Just wait and see.**

Myth: I do not make enough money for a budget to work.

Fact: As we saw earlier with my high school budget example, a budget is crucial for people in every walk of life. I will repeat: **I feel 1000% that a budget is necessary for financial success in every person. To be successful with your money, you have to understand your money, the decisions you make with your money, and why you make them.** Your budget can help you do that. I once worked with a woman who, after bills, had less than a $300 dollars a month to live off of. She still needs a budget. She had a lot to learn about her spending habits. **Change your mindset, change your situation. Make a budget!**

Myth: I do not know how to make a budget and/or I am afraid I will do it wrong, so I just won't/don't do it.

Fact: This one is a frequent flyer! I recently did a lot of "firsts", including writing this publication, all where I had no prior knowledge. I too was afraid, but I had the interest and the desire, so I jumped in. I might do it wrong, but it can be fixed. A budget is no different and let me share something with you: **If you make a budget and try your hardest to follow it, you will most likely be doing much better than you have been doing,** without a budget and tracking system. What if you fail one month? Try again! It usually takes 3 months to get a good budget settled where it is easy each month. **Don't give up. Anything worth doing is hard and this sure is. This, my friend, is the first step.**

Have I dispelled any myths and potentially any wrongdoings in your mind? Then let's move forward.

What happens when people do not have budgets?

- Money comes in and money goes out, there is no relationship with money.
- Most likely an inability to save or an inability to save <u>as much</u> as you would like or your income is able to do.
- Overspending in categories that are flexible like eating out, groceries, entertainment, household items, fun categories, etc.
- Lacking an understanding or education about the foundations of money.
- Hard to make or meet set financial goals without the first step to get there (The budget establishes the foundation for the building blocks!)
- You do the same things every months, thinking you will get a different result (insanity, right?)

I recently surveyed people who budget and the results are in.

People who budget had this to say:

Liberating. When you know where your money is coming from and where your money is going it lifts such an emotional weight to know that, even if things don't look pretty now, that it's going to be alright if you stick with it. Katie, IN

Sometimes I hate it because I'm the free spirit. Sometimes I love it because it makes me feel more in control and secure about my finances. Amanda, MN

I absolutely hate that I have to be responsible and my budget brings that to light. It's much more fun to go out and enjoy my hobbies but much more emotionally peaceful to be responsible. Megan, CO

It is a love hate triangle with myself. I hate it because I am THAT free spirit in every fiber of my being. I love it because of the success we have had and now are able to do so much MORE within our budget! Kate, VA

Now, I can rest assured knowing 1) our bills are paid, and 2) we are paying off our debts with intentionality, not just the minimum payments like before. Plus, when I go shopping it's nice to not feel bad about spending, because we budgeted for it. Kaitlyn, KY

It is surprisingly freeing. I feel less stressed about small purchases because I know exactly where the money is coming from & how much I have allotted for that category for the month. It also helps me make better decisions & avoid impulse buys. I feel like I am empowered. Dana, NC

I love living on a budget because it makes me appreciate people and nature, not "things" and when I do buy things, I really enjoy them. Jennifer, VA

Money is where you say it is if you say that a budget is important enough and you set priorities for your money. Spender (free spirit) or Saver (nerd), as my mentor, Dave Ramsey, coined, both can agree on the **important powers a budget can have on your marriage, your money and your household.**

Okay, we are almost done with the "mind blowing, brain changing, why-haven't-I-done-this-before, where I do I get one of these budget things" information phase and getting on to the planning-and-reflection part, ultimately gliding into the work opportunity. However, before I do, I want to cover one last important subject.

Bankruptcy. Not in detail, my goodness. How awful would I be if after I painted a clear picture of the importance of a budget to your financial future, to then start a conversation about bankruptcy? What I really want to talk about is what a person who files bankruptcy, in general, looks like from a financial perspective, based on my experience. My hope is that this paints a picture of one side of the financial-success spectrum that you can keep in the back of your mind as you are moving out of information phase and into the planning-and-reflection phase.

Again, this is from my experience that I mold a profile of a person who files bankruptcy. They not only file with limited bankruptcy education, but also without any basic financial education; budget, savings, credit, mortgage, and so on. They explain that they took out loans, credit cards, or mortgages without any information or knowledge on payments or interest rates. **They have no budget, usually have never had one, and do not know where to start.** They verbalize they do not lack income, but might actually have substantial income, as well as the inability to manage it, the lack of education, and the lack of budget.

As we head into planning and reflection, I want you to keep one very important thing in mind; if you are married, *I strongly suggest that you do all planning, reflecting and financial work with your spouse.* Making good choices and making decisions for your household needs to be done together. I will cover this in a minute, **but do not even take a step into the next line of this book without your partner.**

PLANNING & REFLECTION

After all of that… you need a budget, right? BUT, how do you get started?

First things first, you have to be in the right mindset to have and use a budget successfully.

Reflection #1: Clearing your Mind

When having and using a budget successfully, it is very important to start with the right mindset. Try the following exercise to help get you ready for success.

In column one, write down everything that keeps you from having, keeping and being successful with your budget. **Do not limit yourself,** keep going until you can think of nothing else.

In column two, write down how you can turn the negative into a positive or the challenge into a solution. Lastly, in column three, **how do you get started in doing that today,** including maybe whose help you may need.

I got you started in the first column.

CHALLENGE	TURN IT AROUND	HOW IT WILL CHANGE
I don't know how to get started	Make the decision, gather education	Finish this book and get started

With the right mindset in hand...errr, mind, it is time to communicate with your spouse.

Of course, we are always communicating with our spouse, but it can sometimes be more difficult with money. I believe the budget needs to be made and reviewed together. Budget tracking throughout the month can be done by one, but you have to communicate about who does that, right? Each household is different on what they decide needs to be communicated about, when it comes to money, but here are some general rules and ideas. Remember, a budget is set up to make sure every dollar has a name. For example: Groceries $X, Eating out $Y, and so on. As a family, we must decide how, when and who pays for what and to make sure we stick to the budget we decide on. Re-read that last sentence. That is very important.

Reflection #2: Communicating with your Spouse (Singles, skip to Reflection #3)

Review the following ideas for ways to communicate about money. Discuss with your spouse what you like or do not like, want to use or not use OR completely different ideas you want to implement. **There is not just one choice per family and there is no good or bad choice.** Happy communicating!

- *As long as it is money that is budgeted for and it has not yet been spent, it does not need to be discussed.*
- *Only one person spends the money, that way there is no confusion on who is spending money.*
- *It is understood who does what purchases, so the budget is followed. One person grocery shops, one person runs other errands etc.*

- *We reconcile our receipts with our budget every few days to double check where we are at and to make sure we are on track.*
- *We do a lot of communicating throughout the day/week so that the person who tracks the receipts can keep track of spending.*

Also, if there is not yet a family budget, some additional decisions will need to be discussed.
- *Who will do the ongoing budget reconciling, throughout the month?*
- *How will decisions be made to purchase items outside of your budget?*
- *When someone wants to make changes to the budget, how will that happen?*

Follow along questions:
- Do you and your spouse already communicate about the above things? If you do not, how will things change in order to start?
- How will you start to implement these changes? How will you make sure they will be followed?

Reflection #3: Accountability Partners (if you are married, skip to #4)

While you will not have the challenge of two people, four hands in the family cookie (money) jar, all other challenges will apply. When will you reconcile the budget, how will you make decisions on when (and how) to make purchases outside of the budget and the best part, **who will hold you accountable?**

The one great thing about having, using and tracking a budget as a couple is the accountability you have from each other. If you are single, you are not "out of luck", **you get to create your own**. In this reflection, it is time to brainstorm, decide and ask your new accountability partner and form a new and powerful relationship.

What to look for in an accountability partner:

1. **Someone you can trust to listen, be there for you, and stick to the rules/plans you put together.** There will be times when you call them or you are with them, when an opportunity arises to purchase something you *really want*. Your accountability partner is there to help you meet your long-term goals and succeed financially, **not always make you happy.** *Pick someone who will do that for you.*

2. **Someone who is on good financial footing themselves.** Not only will they provide good advice (when you ask for it) but they will also know the true importance of what you are doing and how difficult it is. This needs to be someone you bounce ideas off of and know if you are on the right track. You might quickly get off the right track with someone who has a different idea in mind. *You know what you really want? To blow your savings on new shoes! WRONG.*

Do you have someone in mind? It is important to note that this person can be ANYONE. Your sister, your friend, your co-worker, your boss, your dog groomer, your neighbor, your best online friend and so on. If this feels like you are **picking someone for something really special, like first for dodge ball,** it should—because it is.

Now.

What the relationship looks like:

1. **You need to open up.** This is very vague but if you are enlisting someone to hold you accountable, *they need to know what they are holding you accountable to.* What struggles do you have? What is hardest for you? The easiest? What are your goals? What do your finances currently look like?

2. **Lay out a plan.** Based on the above, what will the accountability look like? Do you need assistance at the end of the month to make sure the leftover money goes to your financial goals, instead of wasteful spending? How about assistance during "impulse shopping"? How about a budget making party at the beginning of the month? **What are your needs and how they can they help *you*.**

Check out additional information about the importance of Accountability partners, blogged about here: http://www.thrivefinancialcounseling.com/accountability-whats-it-all-about/ then twitter me your feedback on why accountability partners are important. Make sure you include **#thriveaccountabilitypartner** in your tweet!

Reflection #4: *(last, but not least)* **Getting through conflict**

Money and marriage breeds conflict through terms like your or my money, right? While taking the next step to learn how to communicate and hold each other accountable, it is very important to learn a new way of talking about money to each other.

Not only do we need to reflect about the way we talk to each other about money but what we do after one of us might say or do something, financially, that causes conflict.

Personally, a majority of our household conflicts were gone after my husband and I started budgeting years ago. Like I have previously stated, it took a few months to even get to a working budget, but each month, in all seriousness, *we made sure we came together fed, hydrated, well-rested and in a good mood to talk end-of-month numbers and next month's plan.* We would also come open-minded and open-hearted. I cannot stress the importance of the first steps *(in good physical and emotional health, open-minded and open-hearted).*

Money is a sensitive subject. Let me give you an example; you come to your end-of-month meeting, ready to follow the steps outlined above and in a few minutes your spouse says,

"I think we should get upgraded phones"

This is a simple statement which leads to a complex discussion, since this is a money discussion. Upgraded phones mean, most likely, the cost of the upgraded cellular phone and the increase in your new bill. The discussion will most likely include questions like: where is that money going to come from? Why do you think we need new phones? Have you done research? What is the cost? That simple statement could turn into a fight that could end the scheduled, happy meeting, even when you came fed and watered!

For this reflection, let's take the same statement (or one that commonly happens at your house) and try some different approaches. What is something you are currently struggling with financially? Reflect using these ideas below:

1. Something we have incorporated into all of our conversations is the **speaker-listener technique**. It is actually quite simple but rarely used. If used during money discussions, before we jump to conclusions or get mad, can allow us to hear and *respond versus react.* Once your spouse speaks, you repeat back what you heard them say. Your spouse responds with, *yes, that is right*, and so on, or, *no, that is incorrect, what I meant to say was XYZ*, and such until a resolution and plan is met. BAM. Communication gold.

2. Regardless, your budget meeting is an **open forum for discussion and planning, no one's ideas are bad or wrong.** Decide, brainstorm, and leave the meeting with a plan for what to do with that idea moving forward. New phones? Maybe the discussion includes reviewing how much would fit into your budget monthly, how much you have now to purchase them or if you need to wait and then making a plan to research.

3. New phones? Sure! Of course! No problem. Where does the money come from? Who cares! There goes your budget plan. New car? Sure! Of course! No Problem! (see where I am

going?) While a budget is a livable, breathing document and changes can be made, **changes need to be made carefully and with consideration**. If there is no room in the budget this month, there might be room next month. If it is a necessity, how can you make changes to move money over for this purchase?

It seems like you are ready to get to work! You have found, planned for, and killed anything keeping you from financial success, communicated with your spouse or accountability partner and learned how to work through financial challenges. Are you ready?!

Is it time to create a budget yet?
Absolutely! About time, right?

BUDGET CREATION

A few tips to keep in mind as you venture into budget creation:

1. **Review your bank statements** when creating your budget. I *think* I do not purchase clothes monthly, but if I review my bank statements for the past month (or three) I will see, on average, I might get a pair of shoes every few months, a shirt another month, or some UnderRoos, so there needs to be a budgeted amount. On the same page, I might think I spent much more on groceries when in reality, it is a lot less. We have a lot going on in our lives that it is easy to forget what we spend on everything. Give yourself a break (and a resource!) to get off on the right foot.

2. **If you add everything up and see there is a deficit, chill.** *The only way to create a surplus is by increasing your income or decreasing your expenses.* If decreasing your expenses is the way to go, *be realistic*. Remember to communicate, using the speaker-listener technique, and walk through all available options and decide as a *team*. I will give ideas for ways to stick to decreased budget categories a little later.

3. **Don't guess.** This goes back to #1... well and #2. *To get started on the right foot, put the right and best of your knowledge into your budget.* With valid information in your budget, your changes will be easier and fewer to make, the next month.

4. **Use a complete budget with all categories**. Many times I work with people who state they have no idea where their money is going as they use a budget and they have plenty of

money left over. Once we get started, their budget only includes their bills: rent, utilities, cell phone, cable/Internet, insurance and debt payments. That is not even half the battle without including the liquid expenses like groceries, eating out, personal care, household goods, lottery, gasoline, alcohol, tobacco, child care… and the list goes on and on.

BUDGET TRACKING

This is the heart of your budget. *A budget without tracking is like deciding to get in shape, formulating a plan, going to the gym, but not checking to see if you're reaching your "getting in shape" goals.* Are you getting that six-pack? Are you able to fit into your skinny jeans? What if you continue to do that same exercise without review to find six months later, nothing has changed? Tracking your progress, reviewing for changes and moving forward on the successful path is necessary, regardless of the goal you plan to achieve.

There are a few different ways to successfully track a budget. Pick one that best suits YOU so that you successfully track your budget each month. Let's review...

Online

www.mint.com

This is a free smartphone and online desktop application that automatically pulls all of your financial information and accounts into one place. You are able to simply categorize all of your tracking areas and when you spend, it will put the spending in the right category. Easy, peazy.

Would you like to track your spending quickly on your smart phone or online, but mint is not for you? Check out options like SavvyMoney, BudgetSimple or My Spending Plan.

Paper and Pen

Old-school paper and pen might be the way to go if you like to see and feel your spending as it happens. The upside is that you will not miss a beat tracking side-by-side with your online banking. This might feel like our "way back when" checkbook register tracking but with categories. What is the down side? You will spend a lot of time nose to the paper with a calculator. I do not recommend pen and paper. If you are, like I recommended, budgeting for all areas of your spending and categorizing spending and tracking, pen and paper is going to make that difficult. Putting your budget spending plan on paper is a great idea though.

Excel Spreadsheet

The allows for the best of both worlds and for the hands on ability of pen and paper where the spreadsheet will do the calculating. You can also set up the spreadsheet where rows are purchases and columns are categories. You have the checkbook register tally to the far right and the category tally at the bottom. Did I lose you? Below is a screenshot of a budget form that originated with my work with United Way of Onslow County's Financial Stability Center reworked and adjusted for my work with my clients. Disregard the "spent" category for the time being. This is a small screenshot of the budget template that is included with the purchase of this e-book, that you can find on my website (www.thrivefinancialcounseling.com) to download! Go to *The Only Budget Book* tab to find a password-protected document. The password is: TOBBThrive.

Monthly Spending Plan (Month of: _____)

Monthly Take Home Income		
Salary/Wages (Business)	$	
Salary/Wages (Spouse)	$	
Social Security	$	
Pension/Retirement	$	
Food Stamps	$	
Alimony/Child Support		
(Unemployment)	$	
Other Income	$	
Total Take Home Income		

Housing Expenses	Budgeted	Spent
First mortgage/rent	$	$
Second mortgage	$	$
Real estate taxes	$	$
Repairs/Maintenance	$	$
HO/Renters Ins.	$	$
Electricity	$	$
Gas	$	$
Water/Trash/Sewage	$	$
Storage Unit	$	$
Alarm System	$	$
Other (trash, HOA etc.)	$	$
Total		

Comm./Entertainment	Budgeted	Spent
Entertainment	$	$
Pocket/Fun Money	$	$
Vacation	$	$
Movies	$	$
Internet	$	$
Cable	$	$
Phone service	$	$
Mobile phone	$	$
Other Entertainment	$	
Other		
Total		

Savings Monthly	Budgeted	Saved
Emergency	$	
Long-term	$	
Retirement	$	
College	$	
Other	$	
Total		

Personal/House Item	Budgeted	Spent
Clothing	$	
Child Care	$	
Health club	$	$
Pet Care	$	$
Pet (Food, Toys etc.)	$	$
Household/Toiletries	$	$
Education/Tuition	$	$
Subscriptions	$	$
Alimony/Child Support	$	$
Gifts	$	$
Alcohol/Tobacco	$	$
Lottery	$	$
Laundry/Dry cleaning	$	$
Giving/Tithe	$	$
Life Insurance		
Other		
Total		

Food	Budgeted	Spent
Groceries	$	$
Eating Out	$	$
Snacks/Sodas	$	$
Work Lunches	$	$
School Lunches	$	
Total		

Medical/Health	Budgeted	Spent
Insurance	$	$
Copayments	$	$
Prescriptions	$	$
Over the counter items	$	$
Glasses/Contacts	$	$
Other	$	$
Total	$	$

Transportation	Budgeted	Spent
Gas/Oil	$	$
Repairs/Maintenance	$	$
License/Tags	$	$
Tolls/Parking	$	$
Bus/Train/Taxi	$	$
Insurance	$	$
Other	$	$
Total		

Secured Debts	Budgeted	Spent
Student Loan 1	$	$
Student Loan 2	$	$
Student Loan 3	$	$
Car payment 1	$	$
Car payment 2	$	$
Car payment 3	$	$
Past Due Taxes	$	$
Medical Bills	$	$
Pay Day Loan	$	$
Other	$	$
Total		

Unsecured Debts	Budgeted	Spent
Credit card 1	$	$
Credit card 2	$	$
Credit card 3	$	$
Credit card 4	$	$
Personal Loan 1	$	$
Personal Loan 2	$	$
Other	$	$
Other	$	$
Other	$	$
Total		

Summary		
Total Take Home (Income) (+)		$
Total Secured Debt Payments (-)		$
Total Unsecured Debt Payments (-)		$
Total Savings (-)		$
Total Remaining Expenses (-)		
Disposable Income		

THRIVE

Remember, choose whatever works best for you - just choose one of them. If you try it for month #1 and it makes it more difficult for you to track, try something different or variations of the option. If you want to use an excel, computer based spreadsheet but you do not the above option? Find another one. Whatever you do, track your spending. **A budget doesn't mean much if it spends all of its time on your refrigerator chilling (pun intended).**

When should you track your spending?

You should be tracking your spending each and every month. If you are reading this and have decided to start your budget next month, then the tracking goes right alongside with it. Tracking is the sidekick of a budget, like Robin to Batman. No joke, it seriously is. It is that important.

Why is it so important to track spending?

I like my analogy from before about getting in shape. How about, eating better? I am in an accountability group for healthy eating. I track my eating and my exercise. I think and review my options for food and when I am going to exercise at the end of the day for the next, to make good choices and make time for exercise. It is the only way that it works for me. I have tried before, more times that I wish to share with you, to decide to eat better and exercise, even create a plan (eat this, do not eat this, exercise this time of the day, X times a week), I close my journal, go to sleep and end up a week later wondering what happened. It is like New Year's resolutions as well.

We never return to our goals. We never review our choices. We do not track our progress. We do not remind ourselves daily of our plans. We do not keep our goals in the forefront of our minds. I was at a wedding recently where I said *no* to wedding cake. *Wedding cake.* This was huge progress to me, in the way of my goals.

I am harping I know, but for good reason.

If we state" I am going to do better about spending less on groceries," we will be disappointed at the end of the month when nothing has changed. Next month we might say "I am going to try again," but what has changed? *We need to put a specific plan together for this action and track the steps we are making towards that goal.* Most of the time, we think we are making progress when we are not. How do we know? **We input our receipts, by category, throughout the month, to see where we stand and what we need to do to stay on budget.**

What if I have issues staying on budget?

First, you are not the only one. Actually, those who stick to a budget without any issue are the only ones. So first and foremost, put that thought out of your mind. Moving on, here are some ideas to help you stick to your budget and financial goals.

A Cash Envelope System: Another ode to my favorite money man, Dave Ramsey, on this budget-keeping tool. Whether you use an actual envelope, a coupon organizer or paper clips, the idea stays the same. The categories you overspend in: eating out, groceries, entertainment or fun money - pull out your budgeted amount in cash every week, two weeks or month and you spend in those categories, only out of those "envelopes". Once that envelope is empty, spending for that month's eating out, for example, is done. The trick here is *to be done*.

I remember once, for example, having a date night with my husband in our living room sharing a subway sandwich and a Redbox movie, since all we had left in our entertainment envelope was $8 dollars. I bet it was one of our favorite dates as it reminded us to stick to our goals, communicate and work together and left us with a pretty interesting date night we will share with our children!

Do not track just once a month. Do not plan to have a budget and track your budget, just to get to the end of the month, enter in all your receipts and see you overspent. Disappointment, for sure. **Tracking at the end of the month is just like not tracking at all**. Decide on what works best for you: every 5 receipts, every Monday, every other day, every Sunday before church - to make sure you do not get overwhelmed with tracking and to give you a chance to get a glimpse at your spending so far. If you are tracking through mint.com or another online program, make sure you do not fall victim to *mint's doing it, I do not need to* and leave it to the end of the month either. Schedule the same time of upkeep and review of categories!

Automatic savings is a GEM! When you have gotten to the point of being able to put money aside for savings each month (first, give yourself a big pat on the back!) make sure you set up automatic transfer of that money into your savings account, each and every month. If not, that money can magically get spent. When it is automatically transferred, it was like it was never there in the first place and your savings goals will be able to grow.

Keep your financial goals and specific budget challenges in front of you throughout the month. Keep your savings goal tracker in your office or in the kitchen to remind you what you are working towards. Communicate with your spouse about how you feel things are going, utilizing specific tools to decrease spending. Money conversations should not take over your life, but they should be a part of your conversations!

Wait. Try waiting before making a splurge purchase. This might be the hardest piece of advice I can give you, **but it will change the way you look at money.** A recommendation I can make is that items that are in the budget, do not need approval to be spent (i.e. you have a grocery budget of $300 a month, nothing has been spent and you need groceries, you purchase them), but what happens when something is expensive (for your standards and budget), does not fit into your budget or is just plain outside of your budget plan? Wait until the next day (or the week, weeks, month...). There is something about making the adult decision to wait on a purchase that either makes the purchase no longer needed or solidifies the necessity. Either way, the wait is powerful.

GOAL SETTING

As you have heard me say already, I believe the budget is the first step to any successful financial goal or plan. I have had many clients say things like:

My goal is to be able to purchase a house in five years.

I JUST want to be debt free.

I want to stop living paycheck to paycheck.

We want to contribute to our retirement plans and children's college funds.

I want an emergency savings account.

All fantastic goals and all attainable, but I strongly believe that none of them are attainable without first a budget. You have to be able to successfully tell your money where to go and have money to put towards goals, like those above.

Utilize an extra awesome goal setting worksheet, like the one below to brainstorm, set and help work towards your financial goals. **I am so excited for you!**

Easy but not Easy Savings: Goal Worksheet

<u>Savings Goals:</u> (i.e. vacation, vehicle, house/down payment, furniture)

Short Term (1 month - 6 months)   Total money needed
Monthly Amount

1.

2.

3.

4.

Medium-Term (6 months - 12 months)   Total money needed
Monthly Amount

1.

2.

3.

4.

Long term (12 months - 3 years or more)   Total money needed
Monthly Amount

1.

2.

3.

4.

<u>Some tips to keep in mind:</u>

1. MAKE goals. Involve them in your budget.

2. The more specific the goals, the better.

3. Review constantly. Ask yourself these questions. Are these still our priorities? Are we going to make our goal with our current plan? What else could we do?

Here are some frequent budget questions that I receive that were not included in this e-book that I just did not want you going without:

What should I include in my budget? I mean, some expenses are so small, or my car insurance I only pay for once a year, or car repairs? Hopefully never, but if I do have to, I have no idea the cost and then it breaks the bank! How in the world do I budget for these things?

Wonderful question and I feel your frustration. Depending on the cost and the number of these expenses each month, I would recommend doing a variety of this. Costs like auto insurance and things we might not think about, like birthday or Christmas gifts, should be added up to yearly cost and divided by twelve and budgeted monthly. **We need to quit being surprised when things happen**, like our family members birthdays, and even vehicle repairs. If we own a car, it is pretty likely something will happen to it yearly, even on a small scale, like tires. If we put aside some money monthly in savings for vehicle repairs, when it is needed, we won't be so stressed out. Take that extra monthly money discussed for gifts, repairs and insurance and throw it in your savings account, to remove when needed.

For the small amounts? *Budget for everything!* Although, do not drive yourself crazy with a *Sponge Bob Square Pants* magazine or Netflix category—throw them into entertainment, in this case.

How do I budget for my commission income, which is never the same.

Another fantastic question! Commission income is what is irregular income just like bonuses, a seasonal job, special or short term pay - anything that is not constant. **Complete and track your budget based on your regular income.** Depending on your income and expenses, start with your necessary, must-have expenses first: rent/mortgage, utilities, food, transportation, clothing and go from there. If you utilize your commission to pay bills, then put all your expenses in over from most important to least and every dollar that comes in, in commission, is put against the list and paid, every month, in that order. If you can pay all your bills off your wages, then every dollar of commission is put towards your financial goals. If you fall somewhere in between where some of your commission is used for expenses, then if and when you hit months where you surpass bills, take on your goals!

Even after all of this, I just cannot make a budget work for me. What can I do?

Thank you for sharing your concern. I think it is important to note (as I have a few times in this publication!) that *you are not the only one who has been frustrated by the budget-making-and-tracking process.* I want to first encourage you to re-read, re-work, and re-try everything in this e-book, focused and encouraged to make it work making sure you have to time to focus on the process. **I also encourage you to always keep trying.** I have never heard anything say to me "budgets are so easy and so much fun!" or any close variation. I believe you have to be realistic about your spending and real with yourself about what you can and cannot do with your situation. If you have not yet made a budget and/or tracked for a month, please take one step at a time towards these goals. If you still need help, please reach out to me. Whatever you do, please **do not choose to not budget**—remember the definition of insanity!

To end, I want to share a story that might sound familiar to a lot of you. A client of mine, and good friend, came to me b*roken financially and emotionally.* She was living on one income with three children under four and a high level of debt. To add, there was a major lack of marital communication about finances. There was *my* money and *your* debt and bad decisions. *There was a lot of work done, planning accomplished and goals set.* My friend and her family moved and months later I received an amazing phone call about their successes. With a limited budget, many stressors, debt and decreased expenses, they stuck to their guns (and their goals), received guff from family members and finally started to make headway! On the call she let me know she started a savings account, paid down two debts and threw extra money at others, and their communication has skyrocketed. Best news of all? They have the opportunity to help others and grow their family—something they would not have been able to do without their successes. What an amazing story for this family, for me to be a part of, and for you to hear.

Blessings to you and yours on this adventure.

Lauren Welch is an Accredited Financial Counselor, a financial counselor and owner of Thrive Financial Counseling. She has clocked many hours working with individuals, children, high schoolers, and families with financial challenges from debt disasters, on the brink of bankruptcy, messy budgets, and educating individuals without any past financial education to grow successfully and believe in themselves as managers of their money. She specializes in working one-on-one with families to come up with money management plans, budgets and debt payment plans that work with each unique family. Lauren has a unique way of looking at financial challenges, opportunities for change, and helping people learn financial skills to last a lifetime.

Currently living in Georgia, Lauren is married to a Marine and has a son. As a mother, she has learned to be patient, show grace, get outside, get dirty, and knows a lot about Batman and Transformers, especially Bumblebee. She actively volunteers inside the military with her husband's unit, finding opportunities to teach financial readiness and through spouse activities, as well as sitting on the Board of Directors with the Military Spouse Business Association, writing for various publications and serving at church.

You can reach Lauren at:
Website: www.ThriveFinancialCounseling.com
Twitter: @thrivefinance
Facebook: www.facebook.com/ThriveFinancialCounseling
E-mail: Lauren.Welch@thrivefinancialcounseling.com